Appletree Guides

BIRDS
OF
IRELAND

GORDON D'ARCY

First published and printed by
The Appletree Press Ltd
7 James Street South
Belfast BT2 8DL
1986

British Library Cataloguing in Publication Data
D'Arcy, Gordon
The birds of Ireland.
1. Birds—Ireland
I. Title
598.29415   QL 690.17

ISBN 0-86281-162-7

Contents

Diver-type Birds 11

Divers and grebes are related and are found in Ireland mainly on coastal waters (divers) and inland or inshore waters (grebes). They eat fish, which they catch by diving from the water surface.

Ocean-going Birds 12

This group contains four related species which spend most of their lives on or over the open sea, coming to land only to breed in colonies on coastal sites.

Long-necked Birds 15

The Cormorant and Shag are closely related and are primarily coastal inhabitants, while the Heron is a long-necked and long-legged wading bird found in a wide variety of wetland habitats.

Swans 16

The swans are the most recognizable of all birds. Their very large size and white plumage make identification easy. Only the Mute Swan is a resident in Ireland; the Whooper and Bewick's are winter visitors from the Arctic.

Geese 19

Geese are large birds which are usually associated with wetlands. They all breed in the far north, particularly in the Arctic. Gregarious and vocal, they are characterized by their line and 'V' shape formations in flight.

Dabbling Ducks 20

Dabbling ducks are also called surface-feeding ducks. They feed mainly on vegetable matter on, or close to, the surface of the water. When taking to the air they rise vertically from the water surface.

Diving Ducks 23

This group of ducks feeds by diving completely beneath the water surface to obtain sub-aquatic food. All have their feet far back on their bodies, an added facility to underwater swimming, and they patter the water surface when taking flight.

Hawk-like Birds 24

These birds are grouped together because of their hawk-like appearance. Only one, the Sparrowhawk, is a true hawk; three others are closely related falcons. All, with the exception of the Cuckoo, are birds of prey.

Game Birds 27

All are 'tight-sitting' birds which use their cryptic plumage as protection against human and animal predators. They are ground birds, favouring a variety of habitats, and 'explode' into the air on being disturbed.

Ground and Water 'Hens'   28

These birds are hen-like in appearance and behaviour. They are all reluctant fliers, preferring to run or swim away when alarmed.

Large Waders   31

This group contains the four sizable wading birds which are widespread in Ireland. All are specialist feeders, probing in soft mud for different varieties of invertebrate food.

Medium-sized Waders   32

The shanks are true waders, having long legs for life in shallow water. The plovers, being less water dependent, may be found in drier situations. All feed by pecking or probing in the soft ground.

Smaller Waders   35

Included here are five of Ireland's best-known small shorebirds. They are mainly found at the coast, and are mostly winter visitors from Northern Europe and the Arctic.

Larger Gulls   36

This group comprises Ireland's larger 'seagulls'. In reality they are commonly found inland too. They are instantly recognizable by their white bodies, grey or black wings and lazy flight. The immature birds are not so easy to identify.

Smaller Gulls   39

Though often called 'seagulls', only the Kittiwake is essentially a 'seagull'; the others are also frequent inland. All are readily identifiable in adult plumage but are perhaps more difficult to recognize in immature plumage.

Terns   40

The terns are close relations of the gulls but are more lightly built, with a streamlined and graceful appearance. They are all summer visitors to Ireland, wintering mainly in the south Atlantic.

Penguin-like Birds   43

This group comprises the auks. The feet of these seabirds are placed so far back that they have an upright, penguin-like appearance on the ground. Auks breed in vast 'bird cities' on cliffs around the coasts. In winter they vacate their coastal breeding grounds for the open sea.

Pigeons and Doves   44

Pigeons and doves belong to the same family. All are ground

feeders which are capable of quick, vertical take-off. They are noted for their tender courtship behaviour and soft cooing calls.

Small Ground Birds   47

These birds are closely related and have in common the fact that they live mainly on the ground and are adapted to running rather than hopping. In addition, they feed mainly on insects which are caught on or near the ground.

Swallow-type Birds   48

These birds are adapted to life in the air, having a streamlined shape, swept-back wings and forked tail. All are long-distance migrants which winter in Africa.

Small Brown Birds   51

These four species have in common their small size, predominantly brownish plumage and diet, which consists of insects.

Thrushes   52

The thrushes are instantly recognizable by their brownish plumage and speckled underparts. The Song Thrush and Mistle Thrush are well-known garden birds found in Ireland all year round. The Redwing and Fieldfare are winter visitors from northern Europe.

Garden and River Birds   55

The Blackbird and Starling are very familiar garden birds, many of which live and breed in close proximity to man. The Dipper and Kingfisher are generally associated with streams and rivers and usually afford only fleeting glimpses.

Small 'Perky' Birds   56

These birds are small but clearly marked and coloured. They are not secretive and perch in obvious places, usually near the ground.

Warbler Types   59

This group comprises very small insect-eaters that move about secretively in foliage and are normally difficult to observe as a result.

Tits   60

This is a group of small birds which are well known for their nimble feeding behaviour and their attractive looks. Although woodland species initially, they have become garden birds as well, and coexist comfortably with man.

Familiar Crows   63

The four crows described – Magpie, Jackdaw, Rook, Hooded Crow – are well known as resourceful and intelligent birds. Unfortunately this has gained them a bad reputation in some circumstances.

Less Familiar Crows   64

The Raven, Jay and Chough tend to shun man and inhabit areas where they can live undisturbed. All have characteristic calls by which they can be identified even without being seen.

Finches   67

This group contains five attractive seed-eating birds. They are primarily woodland or open country species but may be found in gardens too. All have distinctive calls by which they may be identified.

Finch-type Birds   68

These are mainly finches or their relatives. Their bills are stout and adapted for feeding on seeds. They are mainly resident in Ireland, and occupy a variety of habitats.

Introduction

About this book

A total of 123 birds has been covered in this book. These are the birds that could be considered to be 'widespread' in Ireland. This does not mean that they are abundant or common, as this depends on the density of distribution. One or two birds have been omitted which could be considered as fairly widespread and one or two have been included which are not yet widespread but look like becoming so.

The birds in the book have been grouped together, generally in threes, fours or fives, under a particular heading. This may be because they are of the same family, are related to one another or simply have something in common. In some the connection may seem a little contrived but it has been necessary, for the sake of compactness, to group them as such.

The text for each of the birds is opposite the colour illustration of the bird. Each is given an English, Scientific and Irish name in that order. The description of each species is brief, concentrating on the important features for identification. Everyday phrases (such as 'rust-coloured' or 'dumpy-looking') are used instead of more formal terminology and the size of the birds, where mentioned, is given as either small, medium or large (small means up to Blackbird size; medium, up to Woodpigeon size; large, greater than this).

The coloured plates show the birds in typical poses. Some flight views are shown also where these are useful for identification. Where there is a significant difference in plumage between male and female, from summer to winter or where the young bird may cause difficulties, these are shown too.

Birdwatching

Birdwatching is good fun. It's a leisure activity for all the family – age doesn't matter. You don't need expensive equipment, your God-given faculties will do! After a while it may be necessary to buy a pair of binoculars but good binoculars can now be obtained quite cheaply. The type you look for are 8 x 40 or equivalent, and there are many good makes.

You can birdwatch anywhere. The back garden, the local wood, the estuary, the coast and the mountains all support birds. It may be possible to see a dozen different kinds in the garden but you may see fifty at an estuary or on the coast.

Take time to identify the different kinds (species) and watch how they live. Birds have feeding grounds, roosting grounds and breeding areas and many also migrate to warmer countries for the winter. If you write down the ones you see in summer and compare those seen in winter it becomes obvious that some of our birds leave in winter but others come here from other countries too.

It adds to the enjoyment of a country walk or a picnic if you take notice of the birds that you see on the way. It's a good idea to take notes and make sketches as well, as this helps to tune the senses. Birdwatching teaches you to look and listen and, perhaps more importantly, to be *aware* of your surroundings. It is by being aware that you can learn to understand nature and how we, as people, relate to it.

So there's more to birdwatching than meets the eye!

Abbreviations

ad: adult
imm: immature
f: female
juv: juvenile
m: male
sum: summer plumage
win: winter plumage

Note: 'immature' refers to *any* sub-adult bird – that is, any bird which has not yet reached maturity and acquired the plumage of the adult bird. 'Juvenile' refers to the first-year state only, during which the chick or young bird wears plumage which it will lose at its first moult.

The Birds of
IRELAND

sum.

win.

Red-throated Diver

sum.

win.

Great-northern Diver

sum.

win.

Great-crested Grebe

sum.

win.

Dabchick

Diver-type Birds

Red-throated Diver *Gavia stellata* Lóma rua

The Red-throated Diver breeds mainly in northern Europe and has a fine plumage with brick-red throat at this time. As a widespread winter visitor to inshore coastal waters it is usually seen in Ireland in its rather drab winter plumage – grey, finely speckled white above; white below and on the face. Though distinctly smaller than the Great-northern Diver, this species is nevertheless quite large. It has a recognizable profile when sitting on the water, with a slightly up-tilted bill position.

Great-northern Diver *Gavia immer* Lóma mór

The Great-northern Diver is, as the name suggests, mainly an Arctic breeder. It occurs as a widespread winter visitor to inshore coastal waters. Only in breeding plumage does it have the fine black and white plumage with barred neck band and back patches. In winter plumage, when it is most common in Ireland, it is, like the Red-throated Diver, quite drab – dark grey above; whitish below and on the face. The head and bill are large and rather angular looking and noticeable from even long range.

Great-crested Grebe *Podiceps cristatus* Foitheach mór

The Great-crested Grebe both breeds and winters in Ireland. The breeding habitat is usually in a lake and the majority spend the winter on estuaries or other inshore waters at the coast. A medium-sized bird with a long neck, this grebe has a strikingly beautiful summer plumage. Both male and female have unusual and elaborate head plumage used in nuptial display. In winter the plumage is dark grey above, white below, on the front of the neck, face and above the eye – a 'ghostly' looking bird. In the rather laboured flight the wings show clear white patches.

Little Grebe *Tachybaptus ruficollis* Spágaire tonn

The Little Grebe, or Dabchick, is very small and dumpy in shape. It is brownish overall with rust-coloured cheeks in summer and yellow bill-gape. In winter it is greyer and paler. It is a widespread breeder in ponds and small lakes with aquatic vegetation. The Little Grebe is hyperactive, diving constantly from the water surface for food. Both this and the Great-crested Grebe have the endearing habit of carrying their chicks 'piggy-back' fashion on the water near the nest. Dabchicks make an unusual 'whinnying' sound at the breeding site.

Ocean-going Birds

Fulmar *Fulmarus glacialis* Fulmaire

The Fulmar is much more 'seagull-like' than the others in this group and is often mistaken for one. The wings are grey as in the gulls but so is the back and tail (white in the gulls). The thick yellow bill and deep-set, dark eye in the heavy white head look different from those of the gulls. The shearing and stiff-winged flight is more like that of the shearwaters than the gulls. The nest is usually on a sea cliff and colonies are found all around the Irish coast in suitable habitats.

Gannet *Sula bassana* Gainéad

The Gannet is one of Ireland's most obvious sea birds, being larger than even the biggest gulls, with brilliant white plumage and black wing tips. Only the adult bird is white: the juvenile is dark grey with fine white speckling, and becomes progressively whiter until the full plumage is attained in its third year. Gannets may be seen fishing anywhere around Irish coasts but there are only a handful of breeding colonies on islands on the south and west coasts of Ireland.

Manx Shearwater *Puffinus puffinus* Cánóg dhubh

The Manx Shearwater is much smaller than the Gannet, with a striking pattern of black above and white below. It has a most recognizable flight. Lines of shearwaters glide close to the waves, showing at one minute black uppersides and at the next, white undersides. They nest in colonies in holes in the ground on cliff tops or similar locations and approach the nests under cover of darkness. As birds of the open sea, Manx Shearwaters are unusual inshore during the winter.

Storm Petrel *Hydrobates pelagicus* Guairdeall

The Storm Petrel is not often seen in Ireland, though countless thousands of them breed in nest-hole colonies in locations along the western seaboard. As with the Manx Shearwater, it comes to the nest at night-time only. It is a tiny bird (about the size of a House Martin) which, having a white rump, is sometimes mistaken for a petrel. The plumage is sooty-black relieved only by the noticeable white rump. During and after storms it may sometimes be seen on inshore coastal waters.

Fulmar

Gannet

ad.

juv.

Storm Petrel

Manx Shearwater

Cormorant

Shag

Grey Heron

Long-necked Birds

Cormorant *Phalacrocorax carbo* Broigheall

The Cormorant is a large, long-necked diving bird, often incorrectly called a 'diver'. It feeds by plunging from the water surface and catching fish, which it swallows on the surface. It is well known for its habit of stretching out its wings to dry while standing at its roost. The plumage is glossy black and in summer the adult has white patches on the face and flanks. The immature birds are much browner than the adults and are pale on the entire underparts. Cormorants nest in colonies on rocky coastal islands and headlands and also in trees in some inland lakes.

Shag *Phalacrocorax aristotelis* Seaga

The Shag is a smaller version of the Cormorant but is strictly coastal. In habits and general behaviour it resembles the larger bird. Its plumage is blackish but has a distinctly greenish sheen and lacks the white patches on face and flanks. The breeding bird sports a tufted crest and bright yellow bill-gape. The immature bird is, like the immature cormorant, pale on the face and the underparts and dark brown on the upperparts. Shags nest colonially, often amongst other seabirds on rocky islets and cliffs.

Grey Heron *Ardea cinerea* Corr riasc

The Grey Heron needs little description, being so well known as to be a favourite subject of Irish folklore. Its singular appearance, both on the ground and in the air, has long drawn the attention of even the least observant of people. It is one of Ireland's largest birds, with a slow, ponderous flight. The legs protrude beyond the tail of the flying Heron but the long neck is tucked back, giving a 'blunt-fronted' look. The plumage is basically grey above and white below but there is a distinctive black streak above and behind the eye extending to a long plume. Long plumes are found also on the neck, breast and back of the adult. The young bird is duller and less strikingly marked than the adult. Herons nest in colonies in the tops of high trees, and sometimes nearer the ground on islands in lakes.

Swans

Mute Swan *Cygnus olor* Eala bhalbh

The Mute Swan needs little description, its beauty having captivated man for centuries. The puffed-out back feathers and gracefully curved neck are well-known features of this bird. The bill is orange and has a black knob at the base. In flight the wings make a tuneful 'wheezing' sound but, as its name suggests, it is more or less vocally silent. The nest is a massive affair, often in an inaccessible spot in a reedbed or along a river. The cygnets are greyish and have an endearing appearance. The adults are less innocent, with aggressive tendencies, sometimes feeding on young birds as well as their more staple diet of aquatic plants.

Whooper Swan *Cygnus cygnus* Eala ghlórach

The Whooper Swan is as large as the Mute Swan but has a less graceful form. A distant flock can look stiff-necked and somewhat angular compared with Mutes. Flocks of Whoopers make, however, the most tuneful sounds, adding atmosphere to stark winter wetlands. The bill is bright yellow with a black tip and the head and bill combined have a wedge-shaped appearance. The young are greyish with pinkish, black-tipped bills. Whooper Swans often feed on river-side callows and other low-lying ground near wetlands, and can look like grazing sheep from a distance. They are fairly widespread visitors to Ireland's larger inland wetlands.

Bewick's Swan *Cygnus columbianus* Eala Bhewick

The Bewick's Swan is like a smaller version of the Whooper Swan. Like the larger bird, the bill is yellow and black but there is less yellow than black. The head shape too is more rounded and less wedge-shaped than that of the Whooper Swan. The young are dull grey with pinkish, dark-tipped bills. The calls of the Bewick's Swan are similar to those of the Whooper but less musical. Wild swans often feed in fields and when Bewicks are intermixed with Whoopers they may be difficult to distinguish. Less widespread than the Whoopers, Bewicks are nonethless regular winter visitors to many of the larger Irish wetlands.

Mute Swan

ad.

imm.

Whooper Swan

ad.

imm.

Bewick's Swan

ad.

imm.

White-fronted Goose

Greylag Goose

Barnacle Goose

Brent Goose

Geese

White-fronted Goose *Anser albifrons* Gé bháneadanach

The Greenland White-fronted Goose is smaller than the Greylag. It is much browner and darker and gets its name from the small white patch on the forehead (though this is absent in the young birds). The best distinguishing features from a distance are the heavy black blotches on the underparts of the adult. In flight it shows less pale-grey on the wings than does the Greylag and the call is a more high-pitched yelping. The White-fronted Goose is now mainly confined to the Wexford Wildfowl Reserve, though scattered flocks overwinter elsewhere.

Greylag Goose *Anser anser* Gé glas

The largest of the geese is the Greylag, so named because of the large, pale-grey patches on the wings. The overall colour is grey-brown, with a large white area beneath the tail and a smaller one on the rump visible in flight. The large orange bill and pink legs are good identification features and are visible from a long way off. When disturbed or in flight, the Greylag makes loud confused honking calls and sounds very like the farmyard goose. The favoured habitats are extensive callows and reclaimed slobland.

Barnacle Goose *Branta leucopsis* Gé ghiúrainn

Almost all of Ireland's wintering Barnacle Geese are found in islands on the west and north coasts, to which they migrate from arctic Greenland each year. The most striking of geese to be seen in Ireland, its grey, black and white patterns of plumage make identification straightforward. In flight, extensive grey patches show on the wings and the flock calls with a noisy yelping. The main habitat is on low, grassy islands but flocks also commute to coastal fields on the mainland.

Brent Goose *Branta bernicla* Cadhan

The Brent Goose is the smallest of Ireland's geese, being not much larger than a Mallard Duck. The pale-bellied form (the form occurring in Ireland) is greyish on the belly and flanks. Brent Geese have small white markings on the sides of the neck and the bill is very small. The young have pale edges to some of the feathers on the back. Flocks of Brents call with a low 'gurgling' noise both on the ground and in the air. They feed on eel grass and other marine plants on coastal mudflats, their primary habitat.

Dabbling Ducks

Shelduck *Tadorna tadorna* Seil-lacha

The Shelduck is Ireland's largest duck – the size of a small goose. It is surprisingly common and widespread as a winter visitor to muddy estuaries and inlets. It is also a widespread breeder in Ireland. The Shelduck is strikingly beautiful, with its black and white plumage, orange breast band, under-tail patch and dark green head. The sexes are alike, though the male is larger and has a conspicuous knob on top of the bright red bill.

Wigeon *Anas penelope* Rualacha

The Wigeon is an abundant winter visitor from northern Europe to Ireland. Flocks are to be found in grassy places alongside lakes, estuaries and some large rivers. On the ground, Wigeon can be quite inconspicuous despite their fine plumage but in the air they are very obvious. The males have large white wing patches and they call continuously with a far-carrying whistle 'whee-oo'. The female is dull and brownish.

Teal *Anas crecca* Praslacha ghlaseiteach

The Teal is Ireland's smallest duck, being little bigger than a Moorhen. In winter it is more widespread and abundant than it appears. The drake is a beautiful but subtly-marked bird with rust-coloured and shiny green head, spotted breast and finely-marked grey body. As with most other ducks, the female is dull and brownish. Teal call from the water with a curious ringing note when anxious. Some Teal stay and breed in Irish wetlands but they are not common breeders.

Mallard *Anas platyrhynchos* Mallard

The Mallard is the common 'wild duck' of the ponds and ditches. A large duck, the male is a fine bird with greyish body, bright orange legs, yellowish bill and curly black feathers above the tail. The female is dowdy brown with a pale eyestripe. Both sexes have a blue-green patch on the wing, edged on both sides with white. The Mallard nests in a wide variety of situations in the vicinity of water.

Shoveler *Anas clypeata* Spadalghob

The Shoveler is roughly the same size as the Wigeon but very different in appearance. The drake is a striking bird, showing a lot of white but with a blackish head, huge bill and obvious rust-coloured sides. The female is dull brownish. Both male and female have conspicious light-blue wing patches, obvious in flight. The Shoveler is a widespread but thinly distributed winter visitor, mainly to freshwater wetlands but also to some estuaries. Very few breed in Ireland.

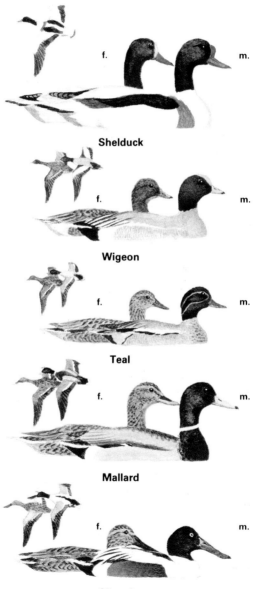

Shelduck

Wigeon

Teal

Mallard

Shoveler

Pochard

Tufted Duck

Eider

Goldeneye

Red-breasted Merganser

Diving Ducks

Pochard *Aythya ferina* Poiseard

The Pochard is quite widespread as a winter visitor to Irish lakes. It is even abundant in some places. Unlike the Tufted Duck, it only rarely breeds in Ireland. The male Pochard is greyish with black breast and rear end. The head is deep rust-coloured. The female is much duller. In flight, both sexes show pale grey wing bars and the flight is rapid and direct like that of the Tufted Duck, to which it is similar in size and shape.

Tufted Duck *Aythya fuligula* Lacha bhadánach

The Tufted Duck is a widespread and, in some places, abundant winter visitor. Although smallish in size, the pied plumage of the males makes them easily recognizable from a distance. Only the male has the tuft on the back of the head; the female is dull, chocolate brown. In flight, a clear white bar shows on the wings of both sexes. Tufted Ducks stay to nest on islets on a few of Ireland's larger lakes.

Eider *Somateria mollissima* Éadar lacha

Ireland's largest diving duck, the Eider is exclusively coastal, favouring rocky areas where it can dive for its favourite foods. The male is unmistakable – a predominantly white sea-duck with a black patch on the sides and other less noticeable black and coloured marks. The female is heavily barred and brownish. Both sexes have a most striking wedge-shaped bill and head. Eiders make strange human-sounding notes when they are displaying.

Goldeneye *Bucephala clangula* Orshúileach

The Goldeneye is a widespread but the thinly distributed winter visitor from northern Europe. The plumage of the male is striking, with predominantly white body and contrasting glossy black head, with a white spot near the base of the bill. The female is dull brownish with a pale neck band. In flight, the Goldeneye is particularly noticeable due to the large white wing-patches and the curious ringing noise made by the wings.

Red-breasted Merganser *Mergus serrator* Síolta rua

The Red-breasted Merganser is a widespread resident in Irish inshore coastal waters and larger lakes. Mergansers have particularly streamlined bodies enabling swift movement underwater. The male is beautifully marked black, white and greyish. The female is greyish brown with red-brown head. Both sexes have very thin red bills. In the air Mergansers fly swiftly and show large white wing-patches rather like those of the Goldeneye.

Hawk-like Birds

Sparrowhawk *Accipiter nisus* Spioróg

The Sparrowhawk is Ireland's most widespread bird of prey. It hunts by flying fast and low and by ambushing its prey. The wings are short and rounded for quick acceleration and to facilitate hunting in confined areas. The tail is noticeably long. The male Sparrowhawk is blue-grey above, barred reddish below; the female is grey-brown above and barred dark below.

Kestrel *Falco tinnunculus* Pocaire gaoithe

The Kestrel is Ireland's most common and widespread falcon, hunting mainly in open country. It hovers as if suspended by an invisible thread, eyes fixed on the ground below, and swoops down to capture its prey. The male Kestral is light red-brown on the back, heavily spotted with black; the head and tail are light blue-grey. The underparts are creamy, spotted with black. The female is larger and duller coloured and is barred rather then spotted.

Peregrine *Falco Peregrinus* Fabhcún gorm

The Peregrine is Ireland's largest and most dynamic falcon. The main prey in the wild are medium-sized birds like pigeons. The Peregrine is heavily built but retains the falcon flight profile. The male is slate-grey above, whitish barred with black below. There are very noticeable black facial marks contrasting with the white cheeks. The larger female is similar but the young bird is browner above and streaked, not barred, below.

Merlin *Falco columbarius* Meirliún

The Merlin is Ireland's smallest falcon but is a highly mobile and effective hunter, being usually found in wild moorland. In winter it often hunts in coastal habitats. The male Merlin is only the size of a Blackbird. It is slate-grey above, whitish streaked reddish below. The female and immature birds are brownish above, whitish streaked dark below. The flight profile is like that of a scaled-down Peregrine.

Cuckoo *Cuculus canorus* Cuach

The Cuckoo is a rather mysterious bird, being much more often heard than seen. It is a summer visitor from winter quarters in Africa. Cuckoos like open country, where they search for the nests of potential foster parents for their offspring. The adult Cuckoo is grey above, white barred with black below and has a long barred tail. The young are rich brown and heavily barred all over. Cuckoos look particularly hawk-like in flight.

m.

Sparrowhawk

f.

m.

Kestrel

f.

m.

Peregrine

juv.

m.

Merlin

f.

Cuckoo

Red Grouse

f.

m.

f.

m.

Pheasant

Snipe

Woodcock

Game Birds

Red Grouse *Lagopus lagopus* Cearc fhraoigh

The Red Grouse is a bird of moorland and bog, where its staple foods, the shoots and berries of heathers and associated plants, are found. The Irish Red Grouse is a medium-sized but very dumpy bird. The male is heavily mottled red-brown, causing it to blend into its heathery surroundings. A bright red wattle is noticeable over the eye. The female is overall paler. On being flushed, grouse appear very dark except for whitish underwing patches. They call with human-sounding notes often described as sounding like the words 'go-back'.

Pheasant *Phasianus colchicus* Piasún

The Pheasant is an introduced bird which has been in Ireland for centuries. The largest of Ireland's game birds, it is so familiar as to require little description. The cinnamon-coloured plumage of the male is heavily spotted with black and the extraordinarily long tail is barred along its length. The female is duller but is also heavily barred and lacks the extra-long tail of the male.

Snipe *Gallinago gallinago* Naoscach

The Snipe is similar to the Woodcock but smaller and camouflaged more for hiding in marshy vegetation than on the woodland floor. The rich brownish plumage is broken up with straw-like streaks. The very long bill is used for probing in soft mud for food. When the marshes are frozen in cold weather, Snipe seek food at springs or even on dry, rough ground. The Snipe's name is descriptive of its sharp call – a typical wetland sound.

Woodcock *Scolopax rusticola* Creabhar

Although the Woodcock breeds in Ireland it is more widespread as a winter visitor. It is not easy to get a good look at this bird for it either sits perfectly camouflaged on the ground amongst dead vegetation or else flies away rapidly through the trees. It is barely medium-sized but is very dumpy in shape with broad, rounded wings and short tail. The bill is very long and straight – ideal for probing in soft ground for food. The rust-coloured plumage is heavily barred and the sexes are alike. Breeding Woodcocks are territorial and the male flies around his 'beat' at dusk.

Ground and Water 'Hens'

Corncrake *Crex crex* Traonach

The Corncrake is sadly decreasing throughout western Europe due to a number of factors. It is now much less widespread than formerly but still breeds in parts of the west of Ireland. It is a medium-sized, brownish bird with rust-coloured wing patches and barred flanks. Corncrakes are rarely seen and identification using the call is reliable. This is a raucous shout – 'aic-aic' – uttered from the cover of a rough meadow or similar location.

Water Rail *Rallus aquaticus* Rallóg uisce

The Water Rail is another secretive bird, much more often heard than seen. The calls are strange and varied, the most familiar being a piglet-like squealing. It is slightly smaller and slimmer than the Corncrake and more attractively marked. The upper parts are red-brown, streaked darker; the face and underparts are slate-grey and there is black and white barring on the flanks. In flight the reddish-pink legs often dangle. The bill is also reddish and is long and slightly downcurved. Although resident in Ireland, Water Rails also turn up at coastal islands on migration.

Moorhen *Gallinula chloropus* Cearc uisce

The Moorhen, known also as the 'Waterhen', is a common and widespread resident, inhabiting wetland locations throughout Ireland. It is a medium-sized, sooty bird with long greenish legs and bright red, yellow-tipped bill. There is white marking along the edges of the flanks and a clear white patch beneath the tail. This is jerked up and down and the head is nodded as it walks or swims. The calls are a series of shrill squawks, mostly uttered from cover.

Coot *Fulica atra* Cearc cheannann

The Coot favours permanent wetlands like larger ponds and lakes. It is larger than the Moorhen, with a bulkier body, and, like the Moorhen, nods its head whilst swimming. Overall blackish in colour, it has a distinctive white bill and shield on the forehead. Coots dive from the water surface for underwater food. On being disturbed they scuttle along the surface of the water in a half-hearted attempt at flight. The Coot calls its own name – a resonant 'coot' – revealing its presence even from the midst of reeds.

Corncrake

Water Rail

Moorhen

Coot

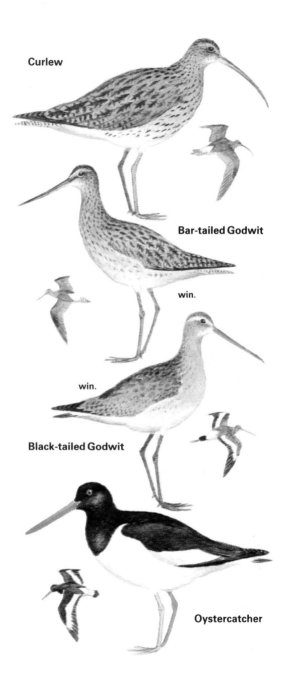

Curlew

Bar-tailed Godwit

win.

win.

Black-tailed Godwit

Oystercatcher

Larger Waders

Curlew *Numenius arquata* Crotach

The largest of the waders is the Curlew – a well-known Irish bird which not only arrives in winter hordes but also breeds in suitable Irish localities. It is a leggy, light-brown bird, heavily streaked and flecked and with a six-inch long downcurved bill with which it probes for food. In flight, the rump and finely-barred tail are white. The wild call from which the name is derived is a familiar sound of wetland pasture and bog, the Curlew's breeding habitats. Curlews feed on agricultural land as well as mudflats.

Bar-tailed Godwit *Limosa lapponica* Guilbneach Stríocearrach

The Bar-tailed Godwit is like the Curlew in many respects. It too is a bird of the open mudflats (though exclusively so), where it probes for invertebrate food using its long, slightly up-turned bill. In winter plumage it resembles the Curlew both on the ground and in flight but it is much less vocal than the larger bird. A widespread winter visitor to Ireland from the Arctic, it is unusual to see it in its brick-red summer plumage in this country.

Black-tailed Godwit *Limosa limosa* Guilbneach earrdhubh

The Black-tailed Godwit is also a winter visitor and passage migrant to Ireland from breeding grounds in Continental Europe. It is similar to the Bar-tailed Godwit on the ground, though the bill and legs are slightly longer, but in flight it has a striking white wing bar and rump and, as the name implies, a black tail. This godwit is not restricted to coastal habitats, but occurs inland in marshy habitats also. In summer plumage (scarce in Ireland) the Black-tailed Godwit is, like the Bar-tailed, reddish in colour, though with black bars on the flanks.

Oystercatcher *Haematopus ostralegus* Roilleach

The Oystercatcher is a large black and white shore bird. It is striking both on the ground and in the air. A broad white bar shows on the wings in flight. In all plumages the bill is bright orange and very noticeable. The legs are pink. The end of the thick bill is quite blunt and used to hammer open the shellfish on which the Oystercatcher feeds. The call is a clear pipe, a familiar sound of the shoreline. The masses of Oystercatchers on Irish shores in winter are mainly visitors from elsewhere in Europe, though many breed in Ireland also.

Medium-sized Waders

Redshank *Tringa totanus* Cosdeargán

The Redshank is one of Ireland's commonest and most wide-spread shorebirds. The majority are winter visitors or migrants from elsewhere in Northern Europe, though they breed in Ireland as well. On the ground the Redshank is a non-descript brownish bird, paler on the underparts but with long, bright orange-red legs. In flight the wings show clear white trailing edges – a very noticeable fieldmark. The call is a clear whistle, 'tiu-oo-oo'.

Greenshank *Tringa nebularia* Ladhrán glas

The Greenshank is slightly larger than the Redshank, with a slightly upturned, not straight, bill. The long legs are grey-green, not orange-red. The overall plumage is greyer, especially in winter plumage. In flight the Greenshank lacks the pale wing-edges of the Redshank, and a long white wedge shows on the rump. The flight call is a clear whistle, 'tu-tu-tu-', quite different from the Redshank's. It is a widespread though thinly distributed migrant and winter visitor.

Lapwing *Vanellus vanellus* Pilibín

The Lapwing is one of Ireland's most familiar waders. The majority are winter visitors, but many also breed in Ireland. The Lapwing looks black and white from a distance but in fact the upperparts have a greenish gloss, visible from close range. A remarkable upward-pointing plume is visible on the head, though this is absent in the young birds. In the air the wings are noticeably rounded and the flight is buoyant. The call is thin and nasal.

Golden Plover *Pluvialis apricaria* Feadóg bhuí

The Golden Plover is another well-known winter visitor to Ireland. It is also a scarce breeding bird. Two races occur here – Northern and Southern. The Southern race is distinguished from the Northern race by incomplete blackish underparts and face. In winter the races are identical – golden-brown above and on the breast, paler below. The call is a rather sad-sounding note.

Grey Plover *Pluvialis squatarola* Feadóg ghlas

The Grey Plover does not breed in Ireland, being a winter visitor from northern Europe to Irish coastal mudflats. In summer it is similar to the Northern Golden Plover but with silver, not gold-flecked, upperparts. In winter it looks like a silvery counterpart of the Golden Plover, except in flight, when the clear white rump and wing bar and unusual black 'armpits' can be seen. The call note recalls that of the Golden Plover but is somewhat extended.

Redshank

Greenshank

Lapwing

sum.

win.

Golden Plover

win.

sum.

Grey Plover

Turnstone

win.

sum.

Knot

win.

Dunlin

win.

sum.

win.

Sanderling

Ringed Plover

Smaller Waders

Turnstone *Arenaria interpres* Piardálaí trá

The Turnstone is a well-known winter visitor from the Arctic to rocky and seaweedy shores. In winter the dull, mottled greys and browns of the plumage merge with the background and Turnstones can be difficult to see well. In summer plumage they are more conspicuous. In flight they are conspicuous in all plumages. The wing pattern is composed of clear black and white bars. The flight call is a series of stuttered notes quite unlike any of the other small waders.

Knot *Calidris canutus* Cnota

The Knot is another Arctic species, which comes to Ireland for the winter months. It occurs mainly on coastal mudflats. At the regular resorts Knots are very gregarious, forming flocks that can be difficult to locate against a background of grey mud. Close up, the Knot can be seen to be a dull grey bird, paler on the underparts. Even in flight it shows no clear-cut identification features. In summer plumage (which is unusual in Ireland) it is transformed into a predominantly brick-red wader.

Dunlin *Calidris alpina* Breacóg

The sparrow-sized Dunlin is an abundant and widespread migrant and winter visitor and breeds in a few places. In winter plumage it is greyish above, whitish below and the bill and legs are black. The bill is quite long and slightly downcurved. The flight pattern has a dark band running up the tail and rump and a thin white wing bar. In summer plumage it is rust-brown above and there is a black belly patch. The call is a thin, buzzing trill.

Sanderling *Calidris alba* Luathrán

In winter plumage the Sanderling is an even paler bird than the Dunlin – silvery-grey above, white below and on the head. In flight the pattern is also Dunlin-like but more striking. The flight call is a clear 'whit-whit', noticeably different from the Dunlin's. In summer plumage the Sanderling is rich brown on the upperparts and on the breast and clear white on most of the underparts. They are widespread migrants and winter visitors.

Ringed Plover *Charadrius hiaticula* Feadóg chladaigh

The Ringed Plover has an unmistakable plumage pattern. The upperparts are brown, the underparts white, but there is a neat black breast band and black facial markings. The legs and bill are orange, the latter with a black tip. In flight it has a wing pattern similar to that of the Dunlin. The flight call is a more tuneful 'prrip'. Ringed Plovers are widespread migrants and winter visitors and breed in Ireland as well.

Larger Gulls

Herring Gull *Larus argentatus* Faoileán scadán

The Herring Gull is perhaps Ireland's commonest and most widespread gull, being found almost anywhere where food is available. The majority of nesting colonies are on coastal cliffs and islands but it has taken to nesting on city buildings and elsewhere. The plumage of the adult is mainly white with grey wings and back. The wing tips are black with white spots. The legs are pink; the bill is yellow with a red spot on the lower half. Juvenile Herring Gulls are grey-brown, heavily mottled darker and the bill is all dark. The immature birds have paler plumage and dark-tipped bills. Herring Gulls call with a well-known high-pitched yelping.

Great Black-backed Gull *Larus marinus* Droimneach mór

The Great Black-backed Gull is easily recognized by its white body, black back and wings and large size. Like the Herring Gull, the legs are pink and the bill, which is larger and more vicious looking than that of the Herring Gull, is also yellow with a red spot on the lower half. The young bird follows the same plumage development of the other gulls but is recognizable in any plumage by its large size, heavy build and massive bill. Great Black-backs nest in coastal localities, often amongst colonies of other gulls. The call of the Great Black-backed Gull is deeper than that of the Herring or Lesser Black-backed Gulls.

Lesser Black-backed Gull *Larus fuscus* Droimneach beag

The Lesser Black-backed Gull is identical to the Herring Gull in size and shape but has dusky-grey wings and back (intermediate in shade between the Herring Gull and the Great Black-backed Gull). The legs of this species are yellow, not pink as in the other large gulls. It is difficult to distinguish between young Lesser Black-backs and young Herring Gulls, especially in the juvenile plumage. Lesser Black-backs are largely migratory and are not usually found in Ireland in winter. The colonies that nest here do so mainly on islets on the larger lakes and, although there are many colonies, it is nowhere particularly numerous.

Herring Gull

ad.

imm.

Great Black-backed Gull

ad.

imm.

ad.

imm.

Lesser Black-backed Gull

juv.

Black-headed Gull

sum.

win.

juv.

Common Gull

juv.

Kittiwake

Smaller Gulls

Black-headed Gull *Larus ridibundus* Faoileán ceanndhubh

The Black-headed Gull in fact has a dark-brown head – and this only in summer plumage. In winter plumage only a blackish spot remains, behind the eye. The best identification feature, however, is the white front to the wings which is an obvious feature in all plumages. Even the young, which are mottled brown above and have a black tip to the tail, show the white forewing. The bill and legs of the adult are red; those of the immature bird are yellowish, the bill having a black tip. The calls are unpleasant, raucous notes and are somewhat like those of the terns. The colony is usually located on a low islet or marshy place and the nests are placed very close together.

Common Gull *Larus canus* Faoileán bán

The Common Gull is badly named, for it is by no means Ireland's commonest gull. It nests in colonies on some inland lakes. In appearance it resembles a smaller version of the Herring Gull, having white body, grey back and wings with black tips. The wing tips are noticeably marked with white and the legs and bill are greyish-green, not pink and yellow as in the larger bird. The immature bird is mottled grey-brown above and the tail has a thick black terminal band. In flight the front of the immature bird's wings are noticeably darker than the rear. The call is a pleasant mewing.

Kittiwake *Rissa tridactyla* Saidhbhéar

The Kittiwake could be described as a coastal counterpart of the Common Gull, being similar in size and general shape. The back and wings are grey, the latter with black 'dipped-in-ink' tips. The bill is dull yellow and the legs are black. There are clear black markings on the upperparts of the immature bird: on the back of the neck, on the tip of the tail and diagonally across the wings. Kittiwakes nest in colonies on sea cliffs and stacks all around Irish coasts, and often associate with other seabirds like auks and Fulmars. The name is derived from the call at the nesting site, which is unmistakably 'kittiwake'.

Terns

Common Tern *Sterna hirundo* Geabhróg

The Common Tern is grey on the back and wings and white over the remainder of the plumage except for a striking black cap on the head. The bill and short legs are red, the former with a black tip. The call is usually uttered on the wing and is a harsh 'k-reeagh'. The young birds are mottled with black and brown on the upperparts, have a partial black cap on the head and lack the deeply forked tail of the adults. Common Terns nest in colonies along coastal sandspits and coastal or lake islets.

Arctic Tern *Sterna paradisaea* Geabhróg artach

The Arctic Tern resembles the Common Tern in many ways. The differences are subtle, the most obvious being a greyish tinge on the underparts, highlighting the white cheeks; the deeper red bill lacking the black tip; the shorter red legs. Despite these differences, identification is difficult, especially when they are breeding together in large mixed colonies. The young are almost identical to young Common Terns.

Sandwich Tern *Sterna sandvicensis* Geabhróg dhúscothach

The Sandwich Tern is the largest of Ireland's terns and is more gull-like than the others. In bulk it is equivalent to the smaller gulls. The tail is less noticeably forked than either the Common or the Arctic Terns. From a distance it looks overall whitish, the back and wings being the palest grey. The black cap on the head is shaggy at the rear. The bill is long, black and yellow-tipped and the short legs are also black. The young are, as in the other terns, mottled on the upperparts. The call is a loud, grating 'kro-ick'.

Little Tern *Sterna albifrons* Geabhróg bhídeach

The Little Tern is much smaller than the others described. The main features are: a white forehead in summer plumage; short yellow legs and black-tipped bill; thin rasping call. The tail is only slightly forked and the flight is noticeably light and dainty. The young have striking diagonal wing markings but are smaller than other species for which they might be mistaken. The nesting colonies are restricted to a small number of beaches on Irish coasts.

Common Tern

Arctic Tern

Sandwich Tern

Little Tern

win.

sum.

Guillemot

win.

sum.

Razorbill

win.

Black Guillemot

sum.

win.

Puffin

sum.

Penguin-like Birds

Guillemot *Uria aalge* Foracha

The Guillemot is the largest of this group and is found in many colonies around Irish coasts. The noise of these colonies has to be heard to be believed – the cumulative effect sounds like weird gargling. The bird itself is warm brown on the upperparts, head and neck; white below and on the edge of the wings. The bill is black and dagger-shaped; the legs blackish also. In winter the Guillemot becomes duller on the upperparts and the face turns whitish.

Razorbill *Alca torda* Crosán

The Razorbill is similar to the Guillemot in size and shape but sits less upright. Razorbills usually breed in association with Guillemots on the sea cliffs. They are black rather than dark brown on the upperparts, head and neck and there are intricate fine white lines on the bill, which is deeper and less dagger-shaped than that of the Guillemot. In winter plumage they become whitish on the face like the Guillemot.

Black Guillemot *Cepphus grylle* Foracha dhubh

The Black Guillemot is smaller and less gregarious than the larger bird. It favours piers, harbours and rocky locations close to the edge of the sea. In summer plumage the Black Guillemot is indeed black but with large white wing patches. The legs and feet are strikingly red. The inside of the bill is also red but the bill itself is black. In winter plumage it looks totally different. After the moult it becomes ghostly white, finely marked with black.

Puffin *Fratercula arctica* Puifín

The Puffin is perhaps the best-known auk. Its dumpy upright stance, black and white plumage and remarkable multi-coloured bill have brought it to the attention of many. It is noticeably smaller than either the Razorbill or the Guillemot and is more stocky in appearance. Besides being coloured with red, blue, white and yellow, the bill is very deep and parrot-like. The winter plumage is much duller. Puffins also nest colonially, but in burrows in the turf at the cliff top rather than on the cliff face itself.

Pigeons and Doves

Rock Dove *Columba livia* Colm aille

The Rock Dove is smaller than the Woodpigeon and lacks the white markings on the neck and wings but there is an obvious white rump patch visible in flight. Two black bars show on the wings both on the ground and in the air and there are glossy green and purple sheens on the head and breast. In the wild form Rock Doves are found along Ireland's rocky coasts. The 'feral' or street Pigeon, so familiar in Irish towns and cities, is descended from Rock Doves that have escaped or have been released from captivity.

Stock Dove *Columba oenas* Colm gorm

The Stock Dove favours agricultural land. It is similar in appearance to the Rock Dove, though slightly smaller and neater. In flight the upperparts show none of the striking white markings of the Rock Dove or the Wood Pigeon, though there is a dark trailing edge to the wings and tail. The head and breast have glossy sheens like those of the Rock Dove. Although less approachable than the other Pigeons, Stock Doves often accompany Wood Pigeons feeding in the fields.

Woodpigeon *Columba palumbus* Colm coile

The Woodpigeon is the largest, most common and widespread of Ireland's pigeons. Large flocks feed together on seeds along roadsides, in fields, etc. and they roost in woods. The Woodpigeon has a strange gliding nuptial flight and often makes loud smacking noises with the wings. The plumage is greyish with a pink tinge on the breast and greenish tinge on the neck. There is a large white neck marking and clear white patches on the wings. The tail, which has a dark terminal band, is often fanned out in flight. As with the other Pigeons, the feet are pinkish.

Collared Dove *Streptopelia decaocto* Fearán baicdhubh

Since its first appearance in 1959, the Collared Dove has become a widespread and common resident. It is found in a wide variety of habitats but it is usually near human habitations. Although it is smaller in body than the other members of the family it has a longer tail than the others. The overall plumage is pale sandy and there are whitish sides to the tail. The undertail region is strikingly black and white, visible in flight. There is a fine black half-collar on the neck from which the name is derived.

Rock Dove

Stock Dove

Wood Pigeon

Collared Dove

Skylark

Meadow Pipit

Rock Pipit

Grey Wagtail m.

f.

Pied Wagtail ad.

juv.

Small Ground Birds

Skylark *Alauda arvensis* Fuiseog stairiceach

The Skylark is Ireland's only widespread and common lark. It is well-known for its remarkable display song in which it ascends vertically into the sky, singing all the while. Larger and more robust than the pipits, it is nevertheless similarly marked with heavily streaked brownish plumage and white outer tail feathers. Skylarks feed on both insects and seeds and gather in flocks in stubble fields in the winter.

Meadow Pipit *Anthus pratensis* Riabhog mhóna

The Meadow Pipit is a common and widespread ground bird, somewhat like the Skylark, with brownish, heavily streaked plumage and white outer tail feathers. It is, however, a more delicate bird, with thinner bill, and lacks the crest on the head. Meadow Pipits call with a distinctive squeak, a very familiar open country call.

Rock Pipit *Anthus spinoletta* Riabhóg chladaigh

The Rock Pipit is an exclusively coastal relative of the Meadow Pipit. It is larger, darker and less noticeably streaked. The outer tail feathers are paler than the others but not white. The bill and legs are blackish, not pinkish as in the Meadow Pipit. The call, too, is a bolder squeak than that of the smaller bird.

Grey Wagtail *Motacilla cinerea* Glasóg liath

The Grey Wagtail is a bird of watery habitats, particularly running streams and rivers. The back is blue-grey; the wings and tail blackish, the latter with white outer feathers. There are clear black and white head markings – more noticeable in the male. The underparts are lemon-yellow, deeper under the tail. In winter the summer finery of the male is dulled and both sexes are alike. The call note has a metallic, ringing quality.

Pied Wagtail *Motacilla alba* Glasóg shraide

The Pied Wagtail is a widespread species as much at home in the country as it is in the town. It is distinctively patterned black and white with a noticeably long black and white tail which is constantly wagged up and down. The female is greyish on the back and the juvenile is dull and less clearly marked. The call is a clear 'chissick'.

Swallow-type Birds

Swallow *Hirundo rustica* Fáinleog

The Swallow is a familiar and widespread summer visitor. It is glossy blue-black on the upperparts; creamy on the underparts with brick-red head patches. There is a row of white spots on the tail which become obvious when the tail is opened and closed. This is deeply forked with very long outer streamers in the adult but not in the young bird. The flock calls with pleasant twittering.

House Martin *Delichon urbica* Gabhlán binne

The House Martin is similar to the Swallow in its glossy black upperparts. The underparts and a neat rump patch are white, however. The notched tail lacks the Swallow's long streamers. The call is a tuneless 'tirrup' – quite different from that of the Swallow. House Martins land on the ground during the breeding season and may be seen collecting mud to construct their unique cup-shaped nests.

Sand Martin *Riparia riparia* Gabhlán gainimh

The Sand Martin is slightly smaller than the House Martin and is warm brown above and white below with a distinct brown breast band. The tail is only slightly forked. The call is similar to that of the House Martin but is quieter. Like the House Martin, this species nests colonially but in holes in banks rather than on buildings. They arrive in Ireland in spring before the other members of the family – often before the end of March.

Swift *Apus apus* Gabhlán gaoithe

The Swift is often taken for a member of the Swallow family but in fact is only a rather distant relative. It is a longer bird, with longer narrower wings and notched tail. Although it is dark brown, the Swift normally appears black. Swifts are so totally designed for life on the wing that they can even roost in the air. The call is a high-pitched rasping or screaming. They arrive later and leave earlier than the others in this group.

Swallow

House Martin

Sand Martin

Swift

Spotted Flycatcher

Tree Creeper

Dunnock

Wren

Small Brown Birds

Spotted Flycatcher *Muscicapa striata* Cuilire liath

The Spotted Flycatcher is a summer visitor to Ireland from African winter grounds but it is rather locally distributed. Insects are caught from a branch or other vantage perch, the Flycatcher flying out quickly and returning to the perch again with the prey. The plumage is grey-brown above, white below with faint marking on the brownish breast. The call is a clear 'tick' and is heard frequently when the young are about.

Treecreeper *Certhia familiaris* Snag

The Treecreeper is often misnamed 'woodpecker' in Ireland due to its manner of feeding – by climbing up the trunks of trees in search of insects in the bark. It is a small, delicate bird with thin curved bill designed more for probing than 'pecking'. The longish tail feathers are stiff and prop the bird against the tree as it climbs. The plumage is streaked brownish above and whitish below. It has a mouse-like appearance as it moves jerkily up and around a tree. The call is a thin and indistinct squeak.

Dunnock *Prunella modularis* Donnóg

The Dunnock, commonly misnamed the Hedge Sparrow (for it is not a sparrow), is a secretive and inconspicuous little bird. It is aptly named dun-ock or *og* (meaning 'little dark one') as it is dark brown, streaked darker on the back and tinged with grey on the head and underparts. The call is a monotonous 'jeep' and the song is an undistinguished little refrain.

Wren *Troglodytes troglodytes* Dreolín

The tiny Wren is one of Ireland's most familiar and certainly one of its commonest and most widespread birds. This energetic little bird with typical cocked-up tail and low buzzing flight needs little description. The plumage is heavily barred on the sides and tail and there is a warm, rusty tinge on the rump and tail. The song is incredibly loud for such a small bird and the call is a sharp 'chick'.

Thrushes

Song Thrush *Turdus philomelos* Smólach

The Song Thrush is perhaps Ireland's finest song bird. Its plumage is warm brown above, pale below, heavily speckled with black. The spots run into one another in dark blotches and streaks. The underwings are noticeably honey-coloured, sometimes visible in flight, and the call is a distinct 'tsip'. Song Thrushes are familiar garden birds, feeding on worms and grubs and using favoured stones as 'anvils' for breaking open snails.

Redwing *Turdus iliacus* Deargán sneachta

The Redwing is the northern counterpart of the Song Thrush. The brown upperparts are darker and less warm in tone. The pale underparts are much more heavily streaked and marked with black. There is a clear yellowish eyestripe. A deep rusty patch is visible on the flanks and is further revealed as an underwing patch by the Redwing in flight. The call is a thin 'ts-eer'. They are abundant and widespread winter visitors, mainly from Iceland.

Mistle Thrush *Turdus viscivorus* Liatráisc

The Mistle Thrush, so named for its liking of mistletoe berries, is larger than the Song Thrush and generally greyer and paler. It is spotted with black on the underparts, the spots being more distinct and less suffused. The tail is also longer and has pale tips to the outer feathers, noticeable in flight, as are the shining white underwings. The call is a harsh rattling but the song is melodious and fluty.

Fieldfare *Turdus pilaris* Sacán

The Fieldfare is about the size of the Mistle Thrush and is similarly proportioned. It is, however, a darker bird on the back, wings and tail. The head and rump are noticeably grey. The underparts are tinged yellowish and heavily speckled and blotched with black. In flight the underwings are shining white like those of the Mistle Thrush. The flight call is a distinctive 'chack, chack'. Large flocks are found in stubbles and other fields during the winter. Fieldfares are abundant and widespread winter visitors from Scandinavia.

Song Thrush

Redwing

Mistle Thrush

Fieldfare

Blackbird m.

f.

Starling ad.

juv.

Dipper

Kingfisher

Garden and River Birds

Blackbird *Turdus merula* Lon dubh

The male Blackbird's matt black plumage and striking orange-yellow bill are so distinctive that it requires no further description. The brownish female is sometimes mistaken for a thrush because of its pale and speckled throat but the differences are obvious from close range. The male Blackbird is one of Ireland's best song birds. Its song is deeper, with less repetition, than that of the Song Thrush, but is nonetheless similar. The alarm call is an excited squawk.

Starling *Sturnus vulgaris* Druid

The Starling is as much at home in close proximity to man as it is in open countryside, and its adaptability to circumstances is one of its outstanding characteristics. Starlings have a wide variety of call notes and as great mimics they often impersonate both animate and inanimate sounds. The plumage is glossy black with fine pale speckling in summer. In winter it is more heavily specked and the young bird is brown rather than shiny black.

Dipper *Cinclus cinclus* Gabha dubh

The Dipper is about the size of a Starling but dumpier in shape. The dark brown and blackish plumage is relieved only by the white throat and breast patch. A rusty band borders the white patch but is by no means easy to see in the field. It is named for its curious and nervous dipping as it stands on a stone in the torrent. The call, which is often uttered as the bird flies with whirring wings close to the water surface, is a ringing 'zit'. The young bird is dull greyish and lacks the adult's white bib.

Kingfisher *Alcedo atthis* Cruidín

The Kingfisher is even smaller than the Dipper but has the plumage of an escaped exotic bird. There are various shades of green and blue on the upperparts. The underparts are orange and there are white and orange patches on the head. The bill is long and heavy for the size of the bird and the small feet are bright red. In flight, which is rapid and direct, the Kingfisher looks like an electric blue flash due to the bright turquoise feathers on the back and rump.

Small 'Perky' Birds

Robin *Erithacus rubecula* Spideog

The Robin is a most familiar garden bird. It needs little description, for its warm brown upperparts and orange-red face and breast are well known. The young bird can be confusing, as it lacks the red breast and is heavily marked with pale speckles. Robins are gardeners' constant companions, sometimes hopping about within arm's reach looking for grubs and insects as they are uncovered. The call is a pronounced 'tick' and the song, which may be sung at any time of the year by the highly territorial male, is a recognizable and pleasant warbling.

Stonechat *Saxicola torquata* Caislin cloch

The Stonechat is an ostentatious little bird which is often to be seen perched on a post or wire fence, or on a sprig of gorse, and particularly in rough ground near the sea. The Stonechat characteristically flicks its wings and tail and calls with short 'chipping' notes, from which the name is derived. The male in summer is a bright little bird with black head, wings and tail and white markings on the wings and rump. The breast is orange. In winter the plumage is duller and the female looks duller throughout the year.

Wheatear *Oenanthe oenanthe* Clochrán

The Wheatear prefers to perch on walls and fences rather than on bushes. It is a summer visitor to Ireland from wintering quarters in Africa and is to be found most commonly at the coast in spring and autumn. The bird itself is at once recognizable by its white rump and black-tipped tail – a striking feature in flight. The wings are blackish and there is a black mark on the cheeks of the male. The male's upperparts are light grey and the whitish underparts are tinged yellowish on the breast. In autumn the plumage is duller, more closely resembling the brown-backed females and juveniles. The call is a sharp 'chack' and the song is a pleasant jangling.

juv. ad.

Robin

f. m.

Stonechat

f. m.

Wheatear

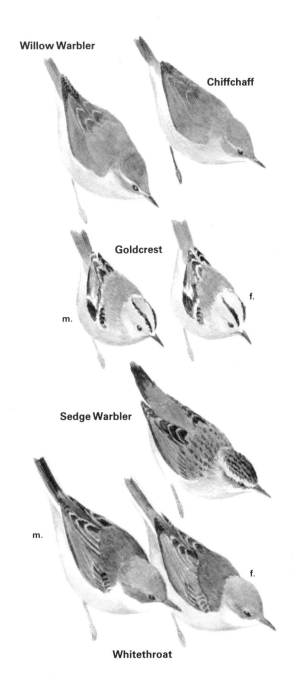

Willow Warbler

Chiffchaff

Goldcrest

m.

f.

Sedge Warbler

m.

f.

Whitethroat

Warbler Types

Willow Warbler *Phylloscopus trochilus* Ceolaire sailí

The Willow Warbler is a common and widespread summer visitor to Ireland. It is found mainly in scrubby habitats but on migration it can be found in all kinds of cover. It is an inconspicuous little greenish bird, paler below and with a yellowish tinge on the breast of the young bird. The call is a distinctive 'lui' and the song is a pleasant cascading warble.

Chiffchaff *Phylloscopus collybita* Tiuf-teaf

The Chiffchaff is, like the Willow Warbler, a widespread summer visitor to Ireland. Very like the Willow Warbler in most respects, it does, however, tend to be more brownish and less yellowish tinged. Other small differences, like blackish, not pinkish legs are less reliable features. The call is similar but the song is completely different. The name is derived from the unmistakable 'chiff-chaff' sung from the tops of trees in summer.

Goldcrest *Regulus regulus* Cíorbhuí

The Goldcrest is closely related to the warblers and is Ireland's smallest bird. The plumage is greenish and whitish beneath and there are black and white marks on the wings. Both sexes show a flash of colour on the top of the head – orange in the male, yellow in the female. The call is a thin mouse-like squeak and the song is simply an extended version of the same sound.

Sedge Warbler *Acrocephalus schoenobaenus* Ceolaire cibe

The Sedge Warbler is a common and widespread summer visitor to Ireland, favouring marshy vegetation. The upperparts are heavily streaked, there is a distinct pale eyestripe and a rusty tinge on the rump. The call is a harsh single note and the song is a loud, varied warbling with harsh sequences.

Whitethroat *Sylvia communis* Gilphíb

The Whitethroat is also a widespread summer visitor, but is nowhere particularly common. Its preferred habitat in Ireland is amongst gorse, brambles or similar vegetation in rough ground situations. The song is a jumbled chattering and the usual call is a low 'churr'. The male is grey on the head; white on the throat; the underparts tinged pinkish; the back brownish tinged rusty on the wings. The female is duller.

Tits

Long-tailed Tit *Aegithalos caudatus* Meantán earrfhada

The Long-tailed Tit is the smallest of the family in body but has the longest tail. It differs too in colour, being mainly pinkish and black above, greyish-white below. There are distinctive double blackish head stripes. The main habitat is scrubland and woods in general. It is less a garden bird than the other tits. Long-tailed Tits feed in little nomadic groups on a wide variety of insects and often join other small birds in the winter. The calls are varied and are reminiscent of those of the Tree Creeper.

Coal Tit *Parus ater* Meantán dubh

The Coal Tit is similar in size and shape to the Blue Tit but is quite different looking. The plumage is mainly grey and brown rather than blue and green and the head is black with whitish cheeks and nape patch. The Coal Tit calls with a 'whistled 'tui' and a variety of other short notes. It is one of the commonest birds of Ireland's conifer plantations, where it feeds on insect life in the canopy.

Blue Tit *Parus caeruleus* Meantán gorm

The Blue Tit is the familiar 'blue bonnet' of the garden which feeds acrobatically on suspended food. It will feed on a wide variety of food, from insects to nuts. The Blue Tit is very small and compact and has a clearly marked head, yellowish underparts and green and bluish upperparts. The call is nasal and buzzing, quite different in sound from the other tits.

Great Tit *Parus major* Meantán mór

The Great Tit is the largest of the family – roughly sparrow sized. Like the Coal Tit, it has a black head with bright white cheeks but lacks the white nape patch. Like the Blue Tit, it is green and blue above and yellow below but there is a thick black band running from the chin to beneath the tail. In general it is a striking and beautiful bird. The calls are similar to those of the Coal Tit but the 'seek-er, seek-er' song is unmistakable. It joins other small birds in winter foraging flocks.

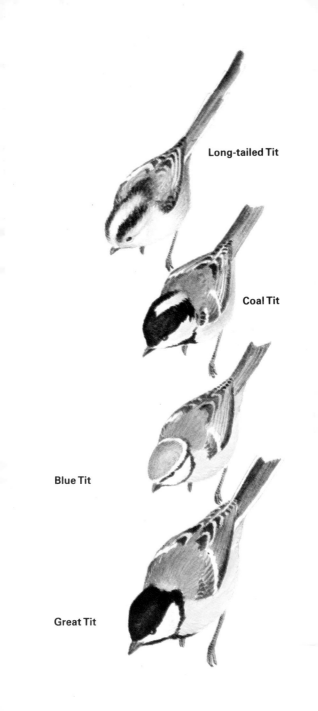

Long-tailed Tit

Coal Tit

Blue Tit

Great Tit

Magpie

Jackdaw

Rook ad.

juv.

Hooded Crow

Familiar Crows

Magpie *Pica pica* Snag breac

The Magpie must be one of Ireland's best-known birds. A clever opportunist, it has learned to exploit food sources of all kinds, including the eggs and chicks of other birds. The noisy chattering, so typical of this species, has become an unpleasant background sound in suburbia. The Magpie is, however, tolerated by many for its fine looks. It is indeed a striking bird, with its pied plumage and ridiculously long tail. There are sheens of green and blue on the tail and wings respectively.

Jackdaw *Corvus monedula* Cág

The Jackdaw is Ireland's smallest crow. It is well known for its rather mischievous appearance and sinister white eye. It is mainly sooty-black, though the sides of the head are greyish. The Jackdaw struts rather than walks and the call is a resonant 'chack'. Like the Starling, the Jackdaw has 'street-wise' habits and coexists comfortably with man. Food sources are varied and tit-bits are found as readily in open fields as they are on the sea-shore.

Rook *Corvus frugilegus* Rúcach

The Rook is a large crow with a more agreeable personality than some of the others. It feeds in the fields but is not above foraging on the shore or feeding on carrion on the roadside. It is very recognizable in breeding season, with its pale feather-less patch at the base of the bill and rather shaggy black plumage. The young bird lacks the bare face patch and can look like an all-black Hooded Crow. Rooks call with a monotonous cawing and the sound at the rookery is noisy and raucous.

Hooded Crow *Corvus corone* Feannóg

The Hooded Crow is less associated with man than the others in this group. Although it does take eggs and young birds it does a valuable job in cleaning up carrion from the roadsides and elsewhere throughout the countryside. The Hooded Crow is so called because of its clearly demarcated black head. The wings and tail are also black but the body is grey. The call is a rather drawn out 'gw-a-ak'.

Less Familiar Crows

Raven *Corvus corax* Fiach dubh

The Raven is a massive bird, being substantially larger and heavier than the Rook or the Hooded Crow. On the ground the most obvious features are the outsized, powerful-looking bill and the shaggy-looking throat. In the air the Raven is longer-winged and longer-tailed than the other crows, the wings showing 'fingered' ends and the tail being quite diamond-shaped. During the breeding season Ravens perform spectacular rolling and tumbling exercises in flight and call with a variety of strange notes near the nest site. The usual call is a resonant 'pruck' or similar croak.

Jay *Garrulus glandarius* Scréachóg

The Jay is about the size of a Jackdaw but much more attractively coloured. Brownish-pink is the general colour but there are black and white patches on the wings and the tail and rump are respectively blackish and white. A 'kingfisher blue' patch is evident at the bend of the wing and there is a black mark on the face at the base of the bill. Jays are excitable birds and when uttering their squawking calls they raise and lower a rough crest on the top of the head. They rarely afford a good view and are most usually seen flying in or around a wood.

Chough *Pyrrhocorax pyrrhocorax* Cág cosdearg

The Chough could be regarded as one of Ireland's speciality birds, as it is more abundant and widespread here than elsewhere in western Europe. It is nevertheless restricted to wilder coastal areas, particularly in the west. It is slightly larger than a Jackdaw, more elegant in shape and with more glossy black plumage. The bill and legs are bright red, the former with a slight downward curve. In flight the Chough has broad, 'finger-ended' wings and, like the Raven, performs marvellous tumbling acrobatics during the breeding season. The name is derived from the wild and evocative call 'keeow' which has a far-carrying quality.

Raven

Jay

Chough

Chaffinch

m.

f.

Greenfinch

Goldfinch

Siskin

m.

f.

m.

f.

Bullfinch

Finches

Chaffinch *Fringilla coelebs* Rí rua

The Chaffinch is a familiar garden bird. The white wing and outer tail markings are features of both sexes, particularly in flight. On the ground the male can be seen to be an attractively coloured finch with blue cap; green and brown on the back and with brick-coloured cheeks and underparts. The female is duller. The call is a distinctive 'pink' and the song is a pleasant jangling.

Greenfinch *Carduelis chloris* Glasán darach

The Greenfinch is even stockier than the bullfinch, with a very stout pinkish bill which will deal with almost any kind of seed. Both sexes are alike in having greenish plumage and bright-yellow flashes on the wings and at the sides of the tail. The young birds are much more brownish, but have the stout beak and general appearance of the adults.

Goldfinch *Carduelis carduelis* Lasair choille

The Goldfinch is a most attractive finch with its black, white and sandy plumage, red face and bright-yellow wing flashes. The beautiful plumage of both sexes and the pleasant liquid notes of the song are well known. It is more of an open country bird than the other finches and will feed avidly on the seeds of thistles and other weeds.

Siskin *Carduelis spinus* Siscín

The Siskin is somewhat like a miniature Greenfinch, being predominantly greenish, but it is more tit-like in its behaviour. The male is clearly marked, with black on the chin, top of the head and streaks on the back. There are yellow flashes on the wings and tail. The female is a duller version of the male. Siskins call with lively twitterings as they move from tree top to tree top, feeding on the cones of a variety of trees.

Bullfinch *Pyrrhula pyrrhula* Corcrán coille

The male Bullfinch is blue-grey above, soft pink below and on the cheeks. There is a black cap on the head and the wings and tail are also black. The female's plumage is much duller but both sexes show a clear white wing-bar and rump in flight. Bullfinches call with a soft 'beoo'. With their stout bill they are well-equipped to deal with seeds of all kinds.

Finch-type Birds

House Sparrow *Passer domesticus* Gealbhan binne

The House Sparrow is familiar to everyone. So well does it coexist with man that it is rarely found far from buildings. Sparrows have seed-eating bills like the finches but will eat almost any household scrap as well. The male is quite well marked, with grey and rust-brown head, brown back and black throat. The female is a rather nondescript grey-brown.

Linnet *Carduelis cannabina* Gleoiseach

The Linnet is a little finch associated most commonly with rough and uncultivated ground. At the breeding site the male sings with an extended and pleasant song. The male in breeding plumage has a red smudge on the breast and forehead; the remainder of the head is greyish and the back is brown. The female is duller. In winter, males and females are alike but both show distinctive pale flashes on the edges of the wings and tail.

Redpoll *Carduelis flammea* Deargéadan

The Redpoll is rather like a small, slim Linnet. In breeding plumage the male has reddish markings on the head and breast. The female is duller, more obviously streaked, and lacks the red smudge on the breast. Both have a black chin mark and clear pale wing bars. Redpolls are highly active feeders. The flock calls with a variety of twittering notes, including a buzzing trill. They are recognizable, even at a distance, by their tiny size and cleft tail.

Yellowhammer *Emberiza citrinella* Buióg

The Yellowhammer is a most attractive member of this family. It is a slim bird with yellow head and breast and red-brown, heavily streaked back. The rump is particularly rusty coloured and noticeable in flight, as are the white outer feathers. The female is a duller version of the male. The usual call is a loud 'chick' and the song sounds like 'a little bit of bread and no ch-e-e-e-se'. The main habitats are gorse-covered commonages and some hedgerows.

Reed Bunting *Emberiza schoeniclus* Gealóg ghiolcaí

The Reed Bunting is similar in size to the Yellowhammer with streaked back and white outer tail feathers, but the male has a black head and throat and whitish underparts. The female is quite different, being generally brown, but is richly streaked with black. The call is a thin 'tiu' and the song is an unremarkable little jangling. The main habitat is in reedbeds or marshy ground but it is also found in scrub sometimes well away from water.

House Sparrow

m.

f.

Linnet

m.

f.

Redpoll

m.

Yellowhammer

f.

Reed Bunting

m.

f.

Index

Arctic Tern 40

Bar-tailed Godwit 31
Barnacle Goose 19
Bewick's Swan 16
Blackbird 55
Black Guillemot 43
Black-headed Gull 39
Black-tailed Godwit 31
Blue Tit 60
Brent Goose 19
Bullfinch 67

Chaffinch 67
Chiffchaff 59
Chough 64
Coal Tit 60
Collared Dove 44
Common Gull 39
Common Tern 40
Coot 28
Cormorant 15
Corncrake 28
Cuckoo 24
Curlew 31

Dipper 55
Dunlin 35
Dunnock 51

Eider 23

Fieldfare 52
Fulmar 12

Gannet 12
Great Black-backed
    Gull 36
Great-crested Grebe 11
Great-northern Diver 11
Great Tit 60
Goldcrest 59
Golden Plover 32
Goldeneye 23
Goldfinch 67
Greenfinch 67
Greenshank 32
Grey Heron 15

Grey Plover 32
Grey Wagtail 47
Greylag Goose 19
Guillemot 43

Herring Gull 36
Hooded Crow 63
House Martin 48
House Sparrow 68

Jackdaw 63
Jay 64

Kestrel 24
Kingfisher 55
Kittiwake 39
Knot 35

Lapwing 32
Lesser Black-backed
    Gull 36
Linnet 68
Little Grebe 11
Little Tern 40
Long-tailed Tit 60

Magpie 63
Mallard 20
Manx Shearwater 12
Meadow Pipit 47
Merlin 24
Mistle Thrush 52
Moorhen 28
Mute Swan 16

Oystercatcher 31

Peregrine 24
Pheasant 27
Pied Wagtail 47
Pochard 23
Puffin 43

Raven 64
Razorbill 43

Red-breasted
    Merganser 23

Reed Bunting	68	Starling	55
Red Grouse	27	Stock Dove	44
Red-throated Diver	11	Stonechat	56
Redpoll	68	Storm Petrel	12
Redshank	32	Swallow	48
Redwing	52	Swift	48
Ringed Plover	35		
Robin	56	Teal	20
Rock Dove	44	Treecreeper	51
Rock Pipit	47	Tufted Duck	23
Rook	63	Turnstone	35
Sand Martin	48	Water Rail	28
Sanderling	35	Wheatear	56
Sandwich Tern	40	White-fronted Goose	19
Sedge Warbler	59	Whitethroat	59
Shag	15	Whooper Swan	16
Shelduck	20	Wigeon	20
Shoveler	20	Willow Warbler	59
Siskin	67	Woodcock	27
Skylark	47	Woodpigeon	44
Snipe	27	Wren	51
Song Thrush	52		
Sparrowhawk	24	Yellowhammer	68
Spotted Flycatcher	51		